First published in India by HarperCollins *Children's Books* 2025
An imprint of HarperCollins *Publishers*
HarperCollins *Publishers* India, Cyber City, Building 10-A, Gurugram, Haryana-122002, India
www.harpercollins.co.in

2 4 6 8 10 9 7 5 3 1

Copyright © Charbak Dipta, 2025

P-ISBN: 978-93-6989-052-1
E-ISBN: 978-93-6989-119-1

All rights reserved. No part of this publication may be reproduced, stored in a retrieval system, or transmitted, in any form or by any means, electronic, mechanical, photocopying, recording or otherwise, without the prior permission of the publishers.

Without limiting the exclusive rights of any author, contributor or the publisher of this publication, any unauthorized use of this publication to train generative artificial intelligence (AI) technologies is expressly prohibited. HarperCollins also exercise their rights under Article 4(3) of the Digital Single Market Directive 2019/790 and expressly reserve this publication from the text and data-mining exception.

Illustrated and Typeset in 14/16.8 Neucha by
Charbak Dipta

Printed and bound at
Nutech Print Services - India

HarperCollins *Publishers*, Macken House, 39/40 Mayor Street Upper, Dublin 1, D01 C9W8, Ireland

*

CHARBAK DIPTA
HJBRL
BASED ON THE NOVELLA BY SUKUMAR RAY

HCCB
HarperCollins Children's Books

CREATOR'S NOTE

In a career spanning just fifteen years, Sukumar Ray pioneered the genre of Bangla nonsense literature, crafting some of the most memorable characters that live on in popular imagination even today.

HJBRL (HawJawBawRawLaw in the original Bangla) remains among my favourite works by Ray, filled with colourful characters and hilarity that is unmatched. I first read it as a child, loving the quirky story and the improbable hijinks that take place. Over the years, as I grew up, my reception of the story also underwent a change, where I picked up on the social and political subtext of the tale. This made me appreciate it, and the work of Sukumar Ray, on a new level.

Now, as the creator of this book, which is a retelling of Ray's original story, I am hoping to introduce a new generation of readers to the mesmerising storytelling that I had experienced all those years ago. As HawJawBawRawLaw was a prose work, its translation into a graphic medium brings in several characters that were not present in Ray's original illustrations. I have also taken some creative liberty regarding names and places. All this has been done to preserve the flavour of the original and faithfully showcase the brilliance of Ray's prolific imagination.

I hope you will enjoy it.

Charbak Dipta
Kolkata 2025

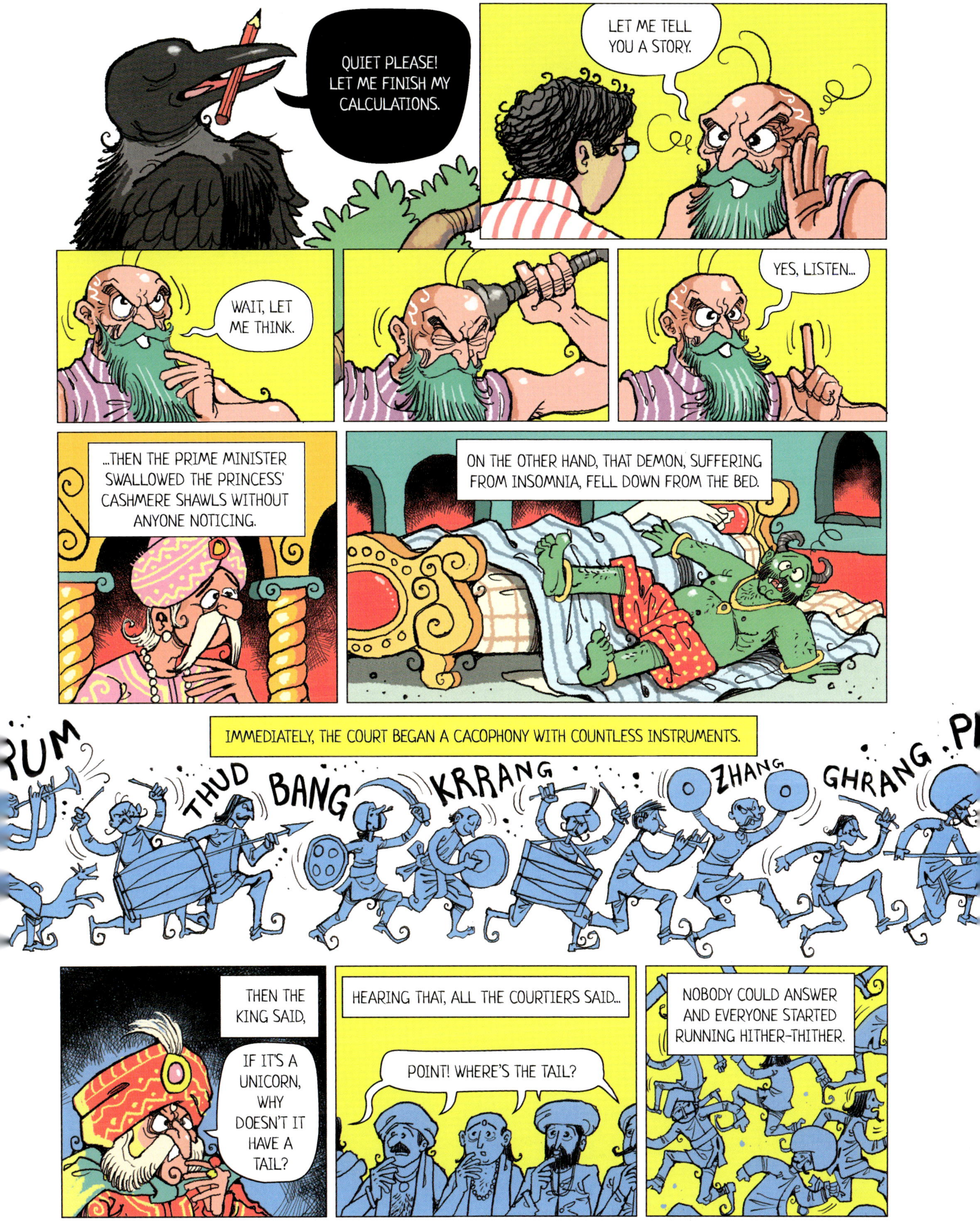

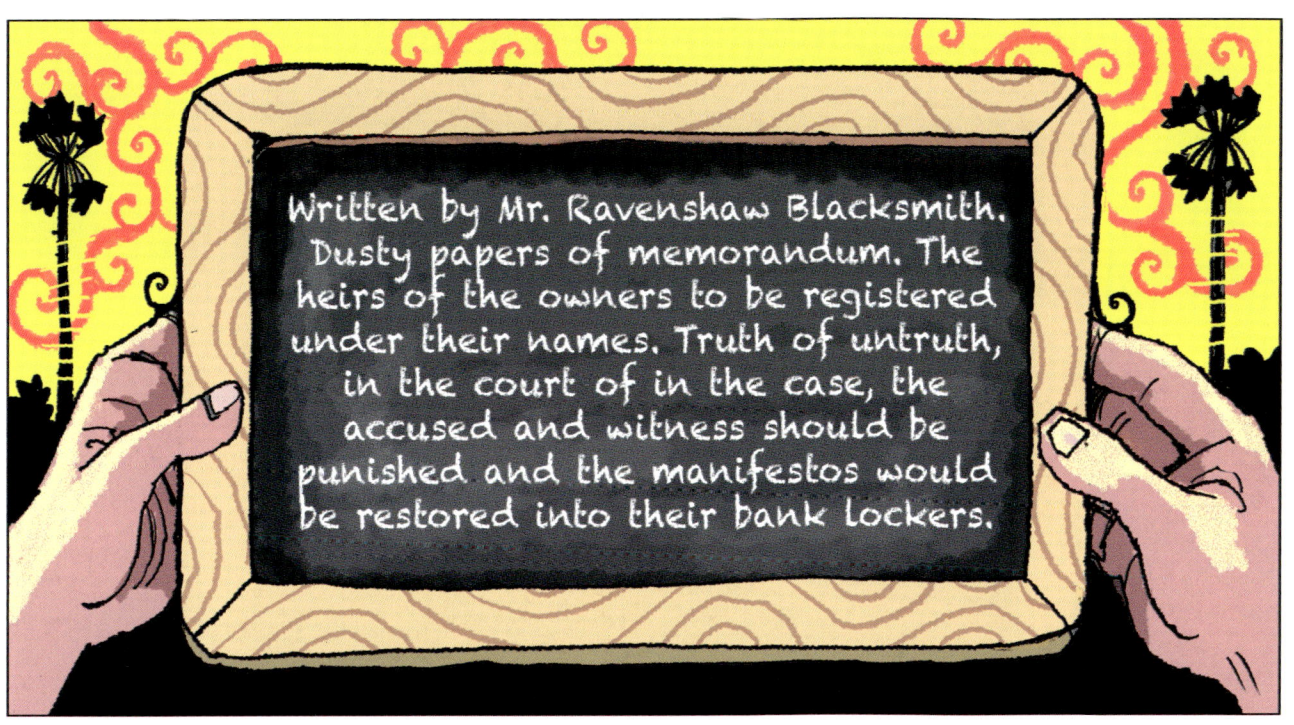

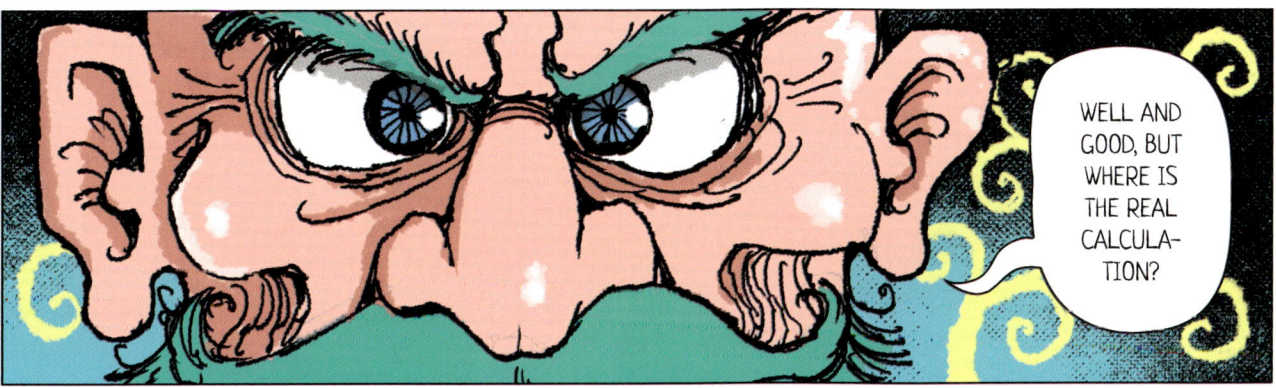

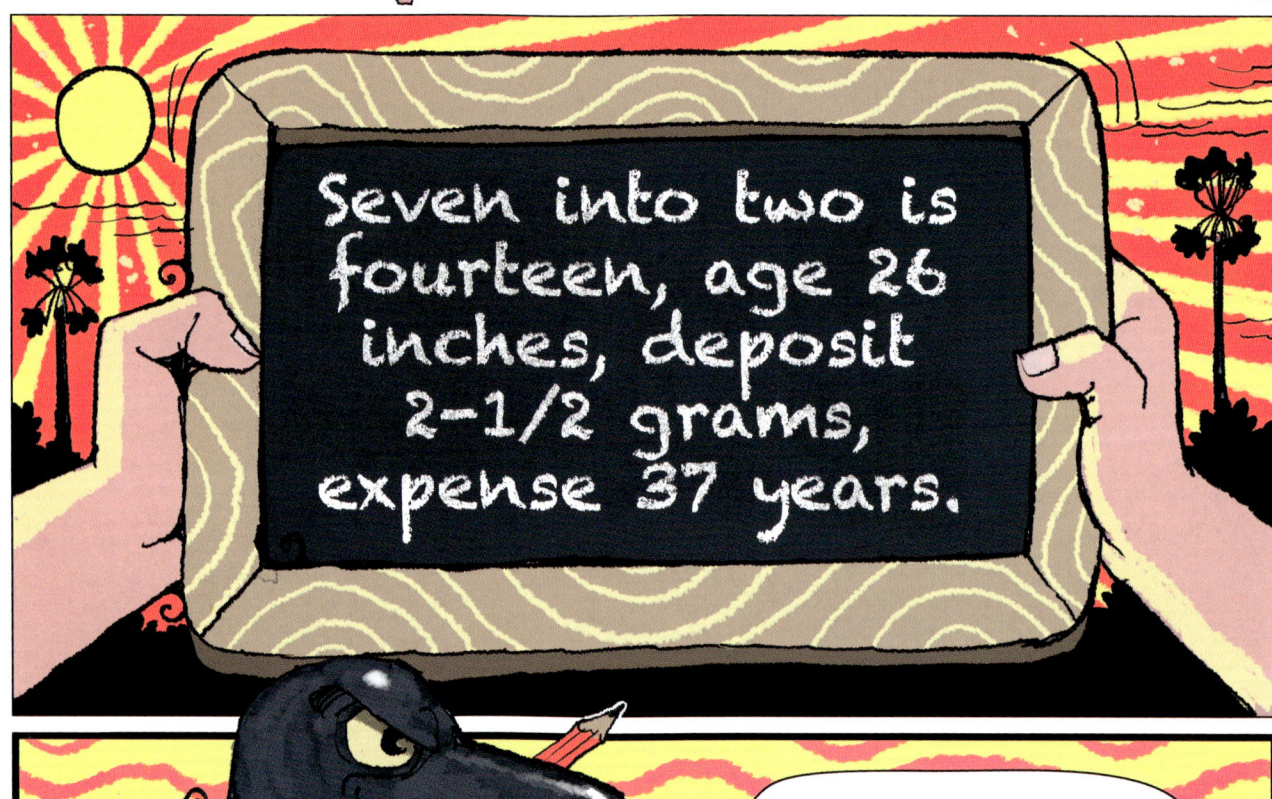

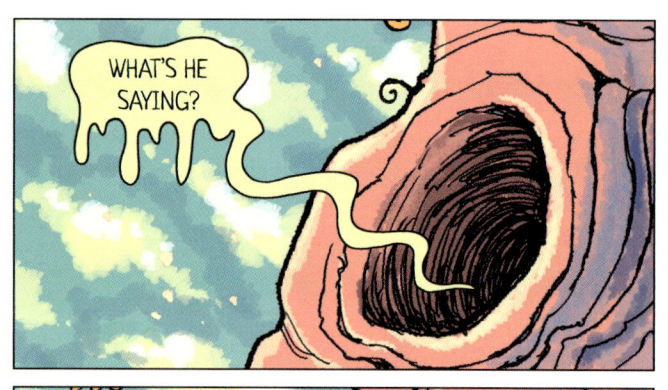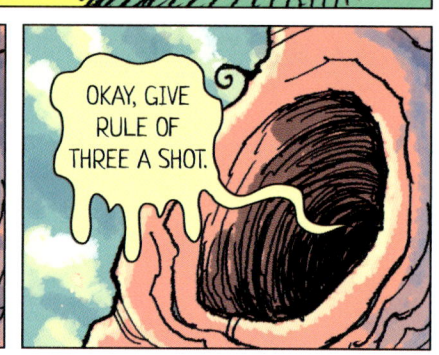

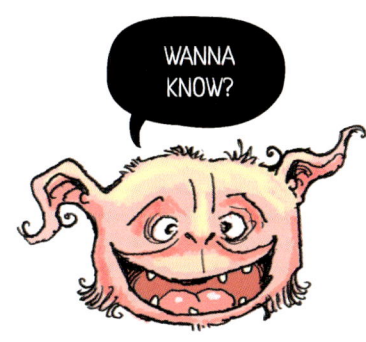

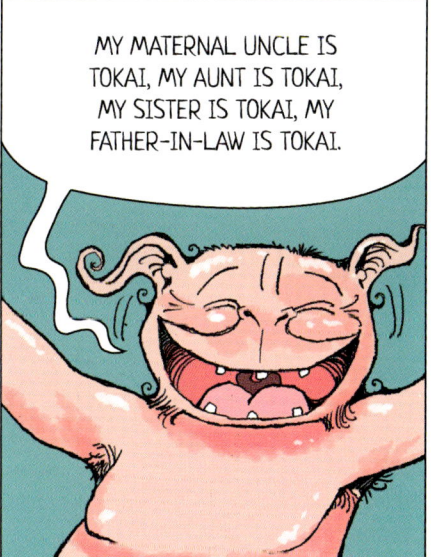